Moses
in Egypt

Canadian edition produced for
Prospero Books
a division of Chapters Inc.

Devised and produced by
Tucker Slingsby Ltd
Berkeley House
73 Upper Richmond Road
London SW15 2SZ
England

This re-telling is based on Exodus 1:8-14:31 of the Authorized version of The Bible

Illustrations by Jan Lewis
Text by Jane Scarsbrook
Designed by Mick Wells and Bob Mathias

Printed in Singapore by Tien Wah Press (Pty) Ltd
Colour reproduction by Bright Arts Graphics, Singapore

ISBN 1 55267 126 7

1 3 5 7 9 10 8 6 4 2

Moses
in Egypt

PROSPERO
B·O·O·K·S
A DIVISION OF CHAPTERS INC.

The Israelite people lived in Egypt long ago.
They had to work hard for the ruling Pharaoh.

This mighty ruler was a jealous man
And he had a truly dreadful plan.

'Egyptians are best! Baby Israelite boys must die!'
So ordered the Pharaoh with a terrible cry.

One woman planned to save her precious babe
And from some reeds, a cradle she made.

Wrapped up snugly so he wouldn't shiver,
She hid the baby down by the river.

Pharaoh's daughter, going for a swim,
Heard the baby crying and went to him.

She pitied the baby left all alone
And, naming him Moses, she took him home.

Moses grew up to be good and kind
But with one great worry on his mind.

'It's a terrible shame,' he thought sadly,
'That Israelites are slaves and treated so badly.'

These angry thoughts got Moses into a fight –
He was trying to protect a poor Israelite.

So Moses was sent from Egypt in disgrace
And worked as a shepherd in a faraway place.

Years later, while Moses was tending his flock,
A bush caught fire and gave him a shock.

God's voice rang out, 'Moses, you will help me
To set all the children of Israel free.'

'And if Pharaoh refuses to let my people go,
Pharaoh and the Egyptians will be brought very low.'

God sent plagues of frogs and flies all about
Until the Pharaoh gave in and let his slaves out.

The Israelites were free at last
And Moses led them out of Egypt fast.

But the evil Pharaoh changed his mind
And sent his army galloping close behind.

Soon the Israelites were in trouble once again –
Stuck between the Red Sea and the Pharaoh's men.

Time was running out, as Moses knew,
So God parted the waves to let them through.

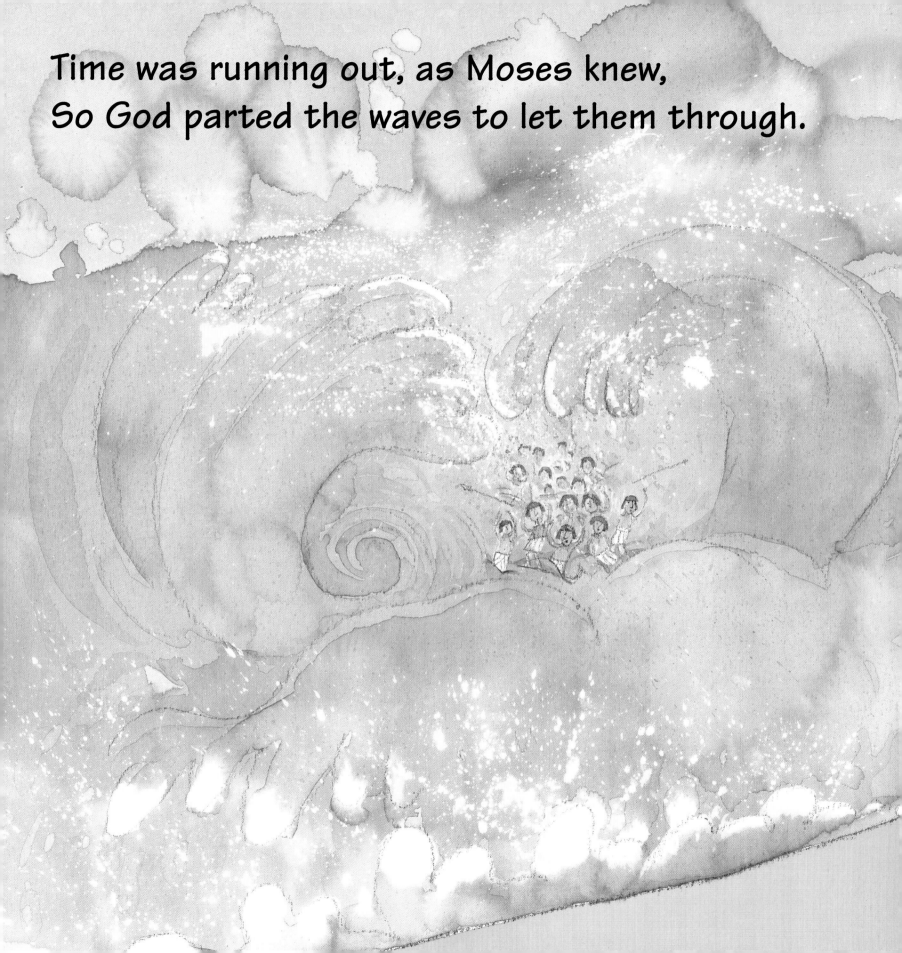

The army drowned and the Israelites were free
To settle in a new land and live happily.

You can find this story in
The Bible
EXODUS 1:8-14:31